Scarred for Life

Martin Travers

Martin Travers has been on the Playwrights' Studio, Scotland mentoring scheme, and on writing attachment with the National Theatre of Scotland.

In 2010 he worked with prisoners to create the script for the large scale *Platform 2:10* project that culminated in four live performances in the chapel at HMP Barlinnie. *Platform 2010* was part of Creative Scotland's ground-breaking Inspiring Change initiative. The script for *Platform 2:10* won a gold Koestler Trust Award in 2012.

In 2011, in partnership with Sense over Sectarianism, *Scarfed for Life* toured secondary schools with a cast of professional actors and members of the Citizens Theatre's Young Company. A new version of *Scarfed for Life* toured Scotland prisons in 2013.

In 2012 his play *Roman Bridge* was the centrepiece of at the National Theatre of Scotland's *Reveal* season.

'eloquent and forceful'
**** *The Scotsman*

'a major new voice might just have been heard'
**** *The Herald*

'the greatest pleasure is Travers' muscular dialogue,
at once flinty and naturalistic and richly lyrical, which
marks him out as a new voice to relish in the future'
**** *The List*

His adaption of Theresa Breslin's *Divided City* was performed at the Citizens Theatre in 2011 and 2012, and in South Lanarkshire and in Derry as part of the Derry/Londonderry City of Culture in 2013. *Divided City* was published by Bloomsbury as part of their Critical Scripts series.

Martin's latest play *Summer Rape Winter Soup* is in development with the Playwrights' Studio, Scotland.

Martin Travers

Scarfed for Life

B L O O M S B U R Y
LONDON • NEW DELHI • NEW YORK • SYDNEY

Bloomsbury Methuen Drama

An imprint of Bloomsbury Publishing Plc

<table>
<tr><td>50 Bedford Square</td><td>1385 Broadway</td></tr>
<tr><td>London</td><td>New York</td></tr>
<tr><td>WC1B 3DP</td><td>NY 10018</td></tr>
<tr><td>UK</td><td>USA</td></tr>
</table>

www.bloomsbury.com

Bloomsbury is a registered trade mark of Bloomsbury Publishing Plc

First published 2013

© Martin Travers 2013

'Burden of the Sash' poem copyright © John Riley 2013

Martin Travers has asserted his rights under
the Copyright, Designs and Patents Act 1988
to be identified as the author of this work

British Library Cataloguing-in-Publication Data
A catalogue record for this book is available from the British Library.

Library of Congress Cataloging-in-Publication Data
A catalog record for this book is available from the Library of Congress.

ISBN: PB: 978-1-4725-3070-7
ePub: 978-1-4725-3202-2
ePDF: 978-1-4725-2698-4

Typeset by Country Setting, Kingsdown, Kent CT14 8ES
Printed and bound in Great Britain

Dedicated to the memory of

Bell, B, and Kate's da Jimmy

Three proud supporters
through the good times
and the not so good times

Introduction

In June 2011, working in partnership with Sense over Sectarianism, the Citizens Theatre worked with eighty young people from four Glasgow schools to find out what they thought about the ongoing problem of sectarianism in society and how it affected their lives. The clear message from the young people was that they had had enough of sectarian behaviour and that adults were the main cause of it in their lives. This response became a central part of the story of the play.

Scarfed for Life was originally performed by members of the Citizens Theatre's Young Company with two professional actors. It played to 900 young people and adults in schools across Glasgow.

This script has been adapted for adults, and this new version of the play was performed in Scottish prisons in March 2013 as part of a Scottish Prison Service Tackling Sectarianism Week.

The publication of the script coincides with performances in nine West of Scotland prisons. After each performance debate is encouraged with the audience about the issues raised in the play. I hope seeing or reading the play gets you talking about the issues too.

John's poem

I met John when he was doing a radio interview with the *Scarfed for Life* cast and have since worked with him on *What's The Story?*, a Citizens Theatre and Motherwell College writing project. When I first read this poem I found it really powerful. It was almost like I could feel the regret coming off the page and wanted many more people to read it. That's why I was delighted when John allowed us to include it here.

Martin Travers

The Burden of the Sash

John Riley

Back for a religious breach
I can't preach
Flag waving, bigotry chants
Sash wearing, I wasn't caring,
I'm on a bigotry journey
I'm guilty and ashamed
People still shiver
At the mention of my name
I can't get out, I'm in pain
I'm trapped in a life I don't want
I can't escape 'cause I'm too deep in the game
A night in the cells, bars as my only guide
Fingerprints, photos, the charge barcode,
On a shuttle bus to the court
I wish I could abort
This place is like a fort,
Sentenced for my crime
As time goes by tick ticking away, I've had enough today
Buckfast has sent me to Alcatraz
The journey to Bar-Hell
I'm achieving in jail
Now I can get space to myself
That's my journey that I regret
There's no excuse for sectarian abuse.

It was part of my life. When I sat down and thought what was going wrong I saw it was a journey that kept taking me back to the same place. To me there's no excuse for sectarian abuse. There's a limit. I wrote 'The Burden of the Sash' to give people an understanding of how sectarianism affects you, others, and society. It's for me to change my ways and help others.

Sectarianism

First Minister Alex Salmond stated:

'. . . the song tells us for Scotland to flourish then "Let us be rid of those bigots and fools. Who will not let Scotland, live and let live". Our new Scotland is built on the old custom of hospitality. We offer a hand that is open to all, whether they hail from England, Ireland, Pakistan or Poland. Modern Scotland is also built on equality. We will not tolerate sectarianism as a parasite in our national game of football or anywhere else in this society.'

An overwhelming majority of Scots support stronger action being taken to tackle sectarianism and offensive behaviour.

The full results show:

89% of Scots agree that sectarianism is offensive

89% of Scots agree that sectarianism is unacceptable in Scottish football

85% of Scots agree that sectarianism should be a criminal offence

91% agree that stronger action needs to be taken to tackle sectarianism and offensive behaviour associated with football in Scotland.

Offensive sectarian language is still used in Scotland on a daily basis, with abusive terms such as 'Hun' and 'Orange bastard' being used negatively against Protestants (or those perceived to be) and others such as 'Fenian' and 'Tim' used negatively against Catholics (or those perceived to be). This reinforces religious and racial stereotypes as well as fuelling the divisions and conflict between the denominations and people of no religious denomination. Children commonly use words without any knowledge of their meaning, but with an understanding that these words are a means by which to insult others.

History of sectarianism

Before the Protestant Reformation in central Europe in the mid-sixteenth century, the vast majority of the people of Europe practised Catholicism. However, the works of these Protestant Reformers found many followers across the continent. John Knox studied these new ideas of how religious worship should be reformed and brought the ideas of these 'protesters' against the Pope and the Catholic Church to Scotland.

This new form of religious observance was found to be very popular in Scotland and at the Parliament of 1560 Scotland was declared to be a Protestant country. This did not mean, however, that Catholicism was eradicated. Those who continued in the Catholic faith, including the reigning monarch, Mary, Queen of Scots, found themselves to be the minority and suffered prejudice and discrimination as a result.

Irish immigration

By the early nineteenth century Scotland was very much a Protestant country. The Covenanting movement, the campaign of Oliver Cromwell, the Battle of Culloden and its aftermath had all contributed to the continued demise of the Catholic faith.

Allegedly at the turn of the ninteenth century, before the Catholic Emancipation Act, there were fewer than forty registered Catholics in Glasgow; at the same time there were almost fifty anti-Catholic organisations; prejudice and discrimination against Catholics therefore continued.

By the 1840s, Glasgow had a thriving economy and was enjoying the benefits of the Industrial Revolution and international trade. Indeed, it is claimed that forty per cent of the ships sailing around the world at this time were built on the Clyde, along with eighty per cent of the world's shipping engines. Not to mention the thriving tobacco trade or the cotton industry.

At this time Ireland suffered the devastating potato famine. The potato crop, which the rural Irish relied upon as both their primary source of food and income, failed over several years, causing widespread starvation and worsening poverty. The Irish people were left to make a harsh choice: to stay in Ireland and risk death by starvation as many of their countrymen were doing, or to emigrate to another country.

The main reason the Irish came to Scotland was to find work. Being poor, these immigrants found accommodation in the slum areas of Glasgow, and in particular the Calton area, which to this day is an area of low life-expectancy and deprivation. The housing was poor but it was all that could be afforded. Here they shared communities with other immigrants from across Europe, as well as the migrant poor from other parts of Scotland who had come to Glasgow to seek employment within the 'Second City of the British Empire'. While the majority were Catholic, the main thing these peoples had in common was poverty.

The Catholics and the Irish faced discrimination in the workplace. Many businesses would not hire them at all. Others were only employed on low wages or as part-time or temporary workers. Signs advertising vacancies would be hung outside workplaces advising that Catholics or Irish need not apply. This led to continued poverty and a hand-to-mouth existence.

Rangers and Celtic

Rangers was formed in 1872 by two brothers, Moses and Peter McNeil, along with two friends. They were all young men from the Kelvingrove and Partick areas of Glasgow. The story goes that the four boys were actually a rowing team who found themselves unable to row as it was a particularly cold winter and the Clyde was frozen over. Looking for something else to do, they saw other young men playing football and decided to form their own team so they could play football when they were unable to row. They initially called the team the Argylls, probably because the McNeil brothers were from the Helensburgh area; however, they changed their name to Rangers in 1873. Moses McNeil apparently read about an English rugby team called Rangers and instantly decided that this was the name for his team. This is also how the confusion about the year of the club's establishment came about. The young men who formed Rangers were all Protestants. At this time in Scottish society, Protestants and Catholics rarely mixed.

Celtic was formed at a meeting in St Mary's church in Calton in November 1887 and played their first match a few months later in 1888. The meeting had been called by a Marist Brother named Walfrid. Brother Walfrid was a schoolteacher who was concerned about the levels of poverty in the Calton area, where children were coming to school hungry and were unable to pay the one penny per week that was required for school dinners. This became a concern, as hungry children struggled to learn.

At this time, Brother Walfrid had also noticed the increasing popularity of football. His idea was quite simple: to form a football team with charitable intentions, charge an entry fee and use the profits to buy food for those who were hungry. As we know, the majority of these poor people in the Calton area were Catholic and many of Irish extraction, so Brother Walfrid chose the name Celtic to emphasise the link between Scotland and Ireland. Unsurprisingly many of the Calton population, who were predominantly Catholic, chose to support Celtic as a result.

Tackling sectarianism

In late 1995 a young man named Mark Scott was walking along London Road in the Bridgeton area with a couple of friends on the way to the train station after attending a Celtic

versus Partick Thistle game. Mark was wearing his Celtic
scarf. Suddenly another young man named Jason Campbell
attacked Mark with a knife and stabbed him in the neck.
The main artery was severed and Mark collapsed, dying
minutes later.

Several factors about this crime shocked the public. The two
men had never met before, so there was no grudge or revenge
in play. There had been no 'name-calling', provocation or
any build up to the attack. It was entirely random. It was
based on the fact that Campbell had been brought up to hate
all Celtic fans and Catholics in general.

In 2001 the partnership Sense over Sectarianism was formed
between Glasgow City Council, Nil by Mouth, Rangers and
Celtic Football Clubs, the Catholic Archdiocese for Glasgow,
and the Church of Scotland.

In 2003 MSP Donald Gorrie raised legislation at Holyrood
making sectarian behaviour and religious bigotry a criminal
offence, resulting in Section 74 of the Criminal Justice
(Scotland) Act (08/04/2003).

Offences aggravated by religious prejudice

The Marches and Parades Regulations were reviewed so that
all demonstrations had to have prior permission of at least
twenty-eight days, and a licence granted by the local
authority in conjunction with the police.

Football Banning Orders were installed so that people found
guilty of sectarian behaviour at football matches could be
banned from games for a period of years dependent on the
level of the offence. This is enforced by the offender having to
attend a local police station at half time when games are taking
place, making attendance impossible, and also by confiscating
passports when the offender's team is playing in Europe.

Local by-laws have been passed so that sectarian and bigoted
paraphernalia, such as offensive scarves and T-shirts etc.,

cannot be sold or worn at football matches. The police have launched their anti-sectarian initiative based around match days and the associated rise in domestic violence around Old Firm matches.

In 2011 the Scottish Government launched new legislation in the form of the 'Offensive Behaviour at Football and Threatening Communications (Scotland) Bill', which strengthened and extended the 2003 Act.

These and various other changes have taken place since the decision was made to tackle sectarianism by the Scottish Government. Perhaps the most important intervention has been the establishment of education both in schools and for community groups across Scotland, but primarily in the Glasgow and travel-to area. Sense over Sectarianism and Education Scotland have launched various educational initiatives such as the novel study *Divided City*, the Communities United programme, and the funding and capacity building for community groups to challenge sectarianism in their local community using community led solutions. This means that the current generation of young people in Scotland is the first to receive this valuable education.

Thanks to

Alison Logan, Kate Black, Neil Packham, Guy Hollands, Mark S. Adams, Rachel Mimiec, Derek McGill, Phil Woodlock, Findlay Laird, Kirsten Sams, Sean Purden Brown, Martin Docherty, Keith Fleming, Michele Gallagher, Owen Gorman, Beth Marshall, Gemma McElhinney, Graham Sutherland, Elaine Coyle, Jacqueline Muir, Natalia Cortes, Tracey Doherty, Andrew F.H. Stuart and wee H.M.H.

Scarfed for Life

Scarfed for Life was first performed at St Thomas Aquinas Secondary School, Glasgow, on 5 September 2011. The original cast was as follows:

Caitlin Fielding
Lynn Kennedy
Leann O'Kasi
Chris McCann
Scott McKay
Ed McKenna
Jack Mullen

Characters

Narrator
Jack, *Celtic fan*
Courtney, *Rangers fan*
Steph, *Jack's mum's boyfriend*
James, *Courtney's dad*
Hugh, *Sheila's husband*
Janey, *Jack's mum*
Janice, *Courtney's mum*
Sheila, *Janice's sister (only referenced)*
Sophie McGregor, *bully and neighbour*
Zumba Instructor
Radio Presenter 1
Radio Presenter 2
Sean Michael, *Celtic fan from Coatbridge*
Radio Presenter 3
Waiter, *Australian*

Set

Seven chairs.

This is a play for seven actors but could be done with more.
All 'Narrator' dialogue should be distributed between the cast
members. The actors never leave the stage but should move
away when not part of the action.

Prologue

Sound of a police siren.

Police interviews and character introductions.

Narrator   This play is called *Scarfed for Life*. One of the main characters in this play is Jack. The bold Jack loves his mammy, Janey. Puts up with Janey's boyfriend, Steph. His best pal's Courtney. Known each other for years. Neighbours. Like brother and sister. Don't fight as much as brothers and sisters. Jack's a Celtic fan.

Jack   Mon the hoops!

Narrator   A bit of an outsider, like Courtney. Jack has – *had* – twenty-twenty vision. His heroes are Kurt Cobain and Jimmy Johnstone.

Where's the bold Jack? He's in surgery.

The **Cast** *set up two chairs in the playing area. These are used by the different characters when being interviewed by the police.*

Narrator   A polis station. Somewhere in the toon. It is eleven p.m. on Saturday night. This is Steph, Jack's maw Janey's boyfriend. You'll work it out later. Well, after all this he can probably kiss the boyfriend status bon voyage. Back to drinkin' buckie in the bus shelter for Steph. Snoop Doggy Dog on the headphones. Puffin' on some cooncil.

All   Snooooooooop!

Narrator   Totally fucked it!

All   Yas!

Steph   Knife ma arse. Big knife? Whit knife! Show me a knife. Show me a witness. Ah wis minding ma ane business. Dane a bit a DIY afore the fitba. You aweright way that? That Hugh is a fanny. It's no finished. That's for sure. Mark my fuckin' words. Whit day ye mean, Am breached!

Narrator   This is James. James is alright. Golf daft.

All   Fore!

Narrator   A good guy. He's Courtney's da. Married to Janice. His daughter Courtney is the apple of James's eye. Good job. Nice house. Wants an easy life. Friendly fella. Widnay day ye a bad turn.

James   Aye, I'm a Rangers man. Born and bred. And aye, that Steph and his rebel tunes gets up the neighbours' noses. Am normally the peacemaker. But. If you're gonnay act like that . . . just . . . don't live here. Go live in the East End. Maybe we just shouldn't mix. It disnay work. You try your best: 'Mornin'! Your team were lucky last night, sir.' But . . . it just disnay work. My cul-de-sac isnay called Rangers Crescent for nothing. Aside that, I mean, a joke's a joke but – you know – whit happened wisnay right. It wisnay right. How's wee Jack dane? I'm awfy fond of him. Any news?

Narrator   Jane. Folk call her Janey. Jack's maw. Loves Steph. Well . . . maybe not after this. Good-looking, but never been lucky with guys. Until she met cheeky chappy Steph. Good company when she's no stressed out. Janey disnay come from the toon. Doesn't get that you're born with it and you die with it. Sectarianism! As Glaswegian as the People's fuckin' Palace.

All   Yowl-day.

Janey   I want to see ma Jack! My wee boy! In surgery! Surgery! Scotland needs to get a grip. You, the police, need to stop all this. Where were you! You're never there when you're needed, are you? You're not police. You're janitors. Men with mops. All you ever do. Mop up. Waste of space. Calm down?! One thing I know. This? This?! This has nothing to do with football. Now if you don't mind I've got a hospital to go to. I have . . . a son . . . in . . . surgery. And an arsehole for a boyfriend. Now open that door before I kick it open.

Narrator   Janice. Works hard. Life's good. Well, apart from the fact her big sister Sheila's married to a prick called Hugh. Janice likes two holidays a year. Keeps fit. Looks fit. Is fit!

A cast member wolf whistles. **Janice** *flips them the finger.*

Janice   Fat chance, arse-crack.

Narrator   Addicted to Zumba. Likes a glass of rosy wine of a weekend, carrot sticks and low-fat hummus. Loves being curled up on the couch with the heating up full bung watching *X Factor* with James and daughter Courtney.

Janice   I can't believe it. I just . . . I just can't believe it. He's a lovely boy. I don't know what Courtney would do without him. Best pals they ur. Two days. That's all we were. Two days at the Hydro. Just to try and get my big sister Sheila away from this . . . this . . . fitba pish. Ahl rip strips aff that James when Ah get my hands on him. Janey will never forgive me. Typical! Stupid wee boy stuff turning nasty again. I've never heard Courtney so upset. My wee daughter. Sobbing. Screaming down the phone. Blood and glass everywhere, she said. Sometimes I think it might just be better to emigrate. We need to . . . this, this stuff? It's like a fuckin' cancer.

Narrator   This is Courtney. Courtney's cool. She's going to do something with her life. Unlike most of us. Probably go to university. In England or Wales. Or America. Or Timbuk-fuckin-tu. She's definitely leaving this country and its pish as far behind her as she possibly can. As soon as she can. Scotland's loss.

Courtney   I'll never speak to them again. Any of them. I'm never going to the game again. Any game. How could they do that? Big tough hard men. Men? Selfish. That's what all this is. All over the city. Selfishness. Women and children scared out of their wits. Scared to go to the shops or the park to play on the swings. Scared of the pubs shutting. Jack and me were minding our own business! Then. All this! Old Firm fans need to grow up or f . . . If it was up to me? I'd ban it. And I love watching Rangers. Supporters? Sport? It may as well be bare-knuckle boxing or dug fighting!

All   Here we go, here we go, here we fuckin' go go!

Narrator   The one and only Sophie McGrrrrrrrrrrrregor. Should have been born a boy.

Sophie McGregor *walks on wearing her skip cap, with her hand down her trackies like a ned.*

Narrator   She's a bobby-dazzler. Bully – and pie-muncher. But I'll say one thing for stinky Sophie: her maw keeps her white trackies glow-in-the-dark immaculate.

All (*sing*)   Blinded by the light!

Narrator   Sophie will not go to university. But she might take a cookery course in Cortonvale when she gets there.

Sophie   Am Sophie McGregor by the way. Might know me. Ahv goat 3,245 . . . 46 Facebook friends. Ye git may? You own Facebook? Naw? Ah saw the lot. The big knife. The daft screaming. It wis me thit phont the polis. Aye, me. That Steph started it. Totally started it. Whit do you expect? He wore a Celtic tap on the day of the Royal Wedding. Awe day. In the pub. Ma da says fuds should get their heed kicked for that kinda patter. Ye git may? Kin ah git ma phone back noo? Naw?

Narrator   And last but not least. Big Hugh. Never been inside a polis station in his life. But inside wan noo, int ye big fella!

We see **Hugh** *with his head in his hands.*

Narrator   He grew up in wan eh they wee toons on the coast. Pretty as a postcard when it's no pishin' way rain. A close-knit community. A wan-team toon. Passionate about his team. A little-known fact about Hugh is he wanted to be a sports physio. Loves sports. Especially fitba. Ended up a plumber. He's the kinda guy you want to fix your burst pipe. Disday cut corners. Widnay rip ye aff. Takes pride in his work. Takes pride in his team. Takes pride in his Scottish Protestant heritage. A wee bit too much pride mibay. Sometimes. But it's awe banter at the end of the day, int it, big fella?!

Scene One

Narrator   Three o'clock Thursday morning. Steph is snoring and farting on the couch. A handful of chips, donner meat and nippy-nippy ring-sting sauce in his fist. His head rests on the remains of an open fat-as-fuck family-size munchie boax. He has nippy-nippy ring-sting sauce in his hair and ear. That's gonnay hurt when he wakes up. The new fifty-inch 3D TV is on. Bought for the fitba and animal documentaries. And a bit of Babe Station when he can get away with it. The message on the screen: 'Celtic Faithful Through and Through: The Tommy Burns Story'. A pirate's chest of pound coins is scattered on the table. Janey stomps down the stairs.

All   Action!

Janey   Steph. Steph. Wake up.

Steph   Whit? Whit time is it?

Janey   Is this it started again? A starter for ten before the match on Sunday. I'm warning you. I don't want you getting arrested. Don't forget you've got a record.

Steph   I wish I hudnay told you about that. I was eighteen. It was nothing.

Janey   Three months in prison for fighting is not nothing.

Steph   It wisnay even a real jail. Ask anybody. Polemont disnay coont!

Janey   Had enough of this last season. You're not playing fair. You don't share a bed with your so-called pals. This is our life together. *Together.* Not you out at the pub and me and Jack sitting here watching *Emmerdale*. You not answering your phone. Me worrying that you've got into a fight again. Or worse. Coming back with another stupid tattoo.

Steph   That's what happens when the bhoys go on the rampage. Champions League fever. Antics. Bit of banter. Leave my tattoo of the Virgin Mary oot eh this.

Janey   Well, as far as I can remember Steph, the Virgin Mary doesn't wear sunglasses. That is a tattoo of Lady Ga Ga you have on your arse!

All (*sing*)   'All we hear is. Radio Ga Ga.'

The **Cast** *clap twice.*

Steph   Ah asked for the Virgin Mary! Ah did!

Janey   You don't even go to Mass.

Steph   Av been meaning to go back. Ah used tay go regular.

Janey   Midnight Mass once a year before your granny died does not constitute regular!

Steph   That's harsh!

Janey   Jack's the teenager in this house. But sometimes I wonder. Your pals rip the piss out of you, Steph, do you know that?

Steph   They're aweright. Ah know they can get a bit mental when they're banging the ching. But they're aweright. My phone ran oot of juice. We goat any juice? Ma ear's throbbin'. And that's no fay listening tay you, before you start. There's something in it. That's dried blood! Might need a doactur!

Janey   That will be nippy-nippy sting-ring sauce you've been sleeping in. Munchy box? You've got a cheek to bring a munchy box into this house!

Narrator   Janey marches into the kitchen past the tile-cutters, bags of grout and the pile of fifty-six chipped or broken tiles that should have been laid before last Christmas.

Steph   There's still some left.

Janey   What the fuck's floating in the fish tank?!

Steph   I thought they might be hungry.

Janey   It that chicken pakora?!

Steph   Any juice?

Narrator   Janey throws Steph a full carton of saver orange juice.

Janey   Help yourself.

Narrator   Steph has the drouf of all droufs.

Steph *glugs from the carton and splutters.*

Steph   That's rank rotten!

Janey   It should be. It's a month out of date.

Steph   Janey. Ah came hame didn't Ah?

Janey   It's three o'clock in the morning. The back door's wide open. A couple of pints?

Steph   Aye well. Didney expect. Ah won on the puggie. Jackpot then the Mega Streak. Deal or No Deal. Humped it. Nearly emptied it. Look! I mean, ye cannay be seen to take the money and run. So I goat the beers in. We won for godsake!

Janey   Your redundancy won't last for ever, Steph.

Steph   Here we go.

Janey   We don't 'go' anywhere any more. That's the problem, Steph. And playing Shamrock Rovers in a friendly is no excuse to get pished on a week night. Sort yourself oot or you'll be waking up in your mother's spare room with that bloody yap of a Yorkshire terrier. Helping it to pick the scabs and skitters out its alopecia!

All   Boke!

Janey   Play fair. Start looking for work. Finish all the wee jobs you've started then left at your backside. Deal or no deal? Us or no us!

Steph   Janey!

Janey   Stay there!

Narrator   She slams the half-stripped living room door and goes back to the cold bed. She wraps herself around the pillow that should be her man.

Steph (*shouts*)   Deal. Us. Promise.

He starts to eat the cold grease-welded mess in the cardboard pizza box.

Am a pure fuckin' dick sometimes.

Scene Two

Narrator   Six o'clock on Thursday evening. Courtney is sitting in her mess of a bedroom reading her horoscope online. *Twilight* posters leer down at her. She has a Rangers scarf above her bed.

Courtney (*reads*)   'Green and red could influence your future this week with Mars drifting into a new phase through Libra. A new pair of shoes might lead to adventure.' OMG that is so spooky! I'll need to get those green-and-red high-tops now. It's a sign!

Narrator   For any auld farts in the audience, high-tops are big leather basketball boots.

Courtney   'Saturday's blood-red full moon and Mars in chaos might bring tragedy.'

Narrator   A Facebook message pops up from – yes, you guessed it, the one and only: Sophie McGrrrrrregor.

Courtney (*reads*)   'OMFG ginger whinger Courtney goes aw Goth. Exclamation mark, smiley face with the tongue sticking out to the side. Liking the new Goth hair, ya bint. Whit a plukey riot. DOG! LOL. Where did she get that stupit hair done? The vet's! Ruff ruff. But whit day you expect fay a fake Rangers supportur that hings aboot way a stupit Fenian. Exclamation mark, exclamation mark.'

Narrator   Courtney stares at the screen. She's just fell into teenage hell.

Courtney   You're the bint, Sophie McGregor. Hope you get skid marks on your white trackies.

She looks at herself in the mirror.

Narrator   A message from Jack pops up.

Jack   Yo! What's happ'nin, Court? What you up to. Question mark. Smiley face.

Narrator   Courtney doesn't answer. She's dealing with a scared feeling that's nipping her eyes and makes things blurry.

Jack   Court. You there?

Courtney   Aye. Coming over?

Jack   Totally. Ma maw gave Steph a pure roastin' last night. Ship up or ship out. LOL. He's been ranting about finishing the tiling, getting feckin' decking! Panic attack material. He only acts like this at New Year when he's pie-eyed. (*Slurs.*) 'New Year, new start Union.' This is gonnay end in disaster.

Courtney   Just come up. Mum and Dad away to Auntie Sheila and Uncle Hugh's.

Jack   Kool kool.

Narrator   Courtney thinks about sending a fuck-you message right back to Sophie but she's scared. Like a wean on her first day at school waiting for her da – and her da disnay show.

Scene Three

Narrator   Six twenty-five on Thursday evening. In the kitchen. Jack stuffs a paperback down the back of his jeans and pulls the chipped white handle of the glass door. Steph stumbles in pushing past Jack. His arms are full of paint pots, brushes, rollers and moth-eaten dust sheets.

Steph   Gone oot, Union? Yer maw's away to the Zumba way Janice.

Jack   I know.

Steph   Was hopin' ye could help me. Ahl get started on the driveway an nat if you finish painting in here? There's money in it.

Jack   Wish I could. But. Canney. Am a teenager. Clumsy. Lazy. A liability in a work environment. Look at the bags under my eyes, Steph man. Need all my energy for Facebook and watching American vampire DVDs. And when I put my arm up in the air the BO is totally horrendous. No kiddin'. Really. Smell me. There's not a deodorant invented that can tackle this affliction. Health and Safety issue, know whit Ah mean?

Steph   Thirty quid.

Jack   As if! A hunner.

Steph   Fuck off! Fifty quid. Two coats.

Jack   A hunner. And I'll paint my bedroom.

Steph   A hunner. Kitchen, your bedroom, Ah pick the colour, and the bathroom ceiling. Two coats. The morra. Cash in hand.

Jack   What's the catch?

Steph   You come way me tay the pub to watch the fitba on Sunday. You will be my get-out-of-jail-free card.

Jack   You're a total jake dog bastart.

Steph   That's ma name, don't wear it oot. Awe come own! It's the first Old Firm game of the season! A ten pinter!

Jack   No chance! The last time we watched the game in the pub you started an argument with a man in a wheelchair.

Steph   He punched me in the haw maws!

Jack   You started it with that Lourdes joke!

Steph   That's a crackin' joke. Janey will let me go if you come way me. You paint. Ah DIY and dig the gairden. Mission accomplished. Halo back in place. Pub. Glug, glug, glug. Hump the gers. Munchy boax. Salt, vinegar, plentay ah nippy-nippy Ring-Sting sauce. Hame. Cans and a cheeky wee huaf. Watch the highlights. Hunner poun'. Cash money!

Jack   Cannay. Promised Courtney we'd watch it here. Let her get away from her mad uncle and his sectarian shouting.

Steph   Sectarianism is a myth. There's good guys and there's wanks. We're the good guys. End of story.

Jack   You're blissfully ignorant sometimes, Steph, you know that?

Steph   What's the point going to a Catholic school if you're gonnay watch the fitba way a hun?!

Jack   What's the point of buying us a new fifty-inch 3D telly for the fitba if you're still gonnay go to pub, git pished and upset ma maw?

Steph   The at-mos-phere.

She sings from the first lines of Russ Abbot's song 'Atmosphere'.

An Ah cannay get a ticket.

Jack   You don't *want* a ticket. You never *want* a ticket. Gone to the game wastes too much drinking time.

Steph   You're coming with me. That wee blue-nose pain in the arse isnay watching her shite team on my Catholic telly and that's final. Day ye want the dosh or no?

Jack   Ahl think about it.

Steph   Whit day ye git when ye cross an orange and a plum? A Rangers fan. Git it?!

Jack   That's as funny as a bullet in the post.

Jack *slams the door.* **Steph** *tries to pull the door open to have the last word.*

Steph   Jack, come back. Where's your sense of humour!

Narrator   Steph kicks an open five-litre tin of purple gloss across the kitchen. Purple gloss everywhere.

Steph   Naw, naw, naw, naw, naw! Ya tinna gloss bastart!

Scene Four

Janey *and* **Janice** *are at Zumba. They work out as they speak. Music plays.*

Zumba Instructor   Come on, girls. Let's make some room for those Christmas calories! Only three months to go before Santa comes down your chimney!

Janice   So to cut a long story short – Sheila's at the end of her tether. Her nerves are shattered. Hugh's never hit her or anything. He's a nice big fella half the year. But when the football season starts: Jekyll and Hyde.

Janey   Hugh seems nice. A bit loud maybe. The nodding British bulldog with the Union Jack waistcoat that sits on the parcel shelf of his car and sings Rule Britannia drives my Steph round the bend.

Janice   They love each other. But she says she can't cope with the upset any more. The lump in her gut she calls it. Walking on eggshells. Rangers win: fireworks at eleven a'cloak on a Sunday night. We get beat: doors get slammed. Dishes get broke. He booted the rabbit hutch the last time. Davie Cooper's no been seen since.

Janey   Davie who?

Janice   The rabbit! Sick of fitba, she says. So. The Hydro for us. Get her away for a bit.

Zumba Instructor   Janey and Janice. Don't think I can't see you talking when you should be walking. If talking burned calories you two would be anorexic.

Janice   Less of your cheek, Freddy. I did the Ten K in the summer. Where were you? Playing kiss, cuddle or torture up The Corinthian!

Zumba Instructor   Bitch.

Janey   This weekend? I'd like to. Teach Steph not to take me for granted. It's really short notice, Janice.

Janice   Short notice? It's all-inclusive! It'll be as good as Take That at Hampden! Just think. Rosé wine. Steam room. Hot stones dipped in lavender oil. Croissants and smoothies for breakfast. Nay ironing. Come back Monday morning. Nails done. Landing strips. The lot! It's like a wee strike without the picket line.

Zumba Instructor   Janice! The naughty step's got your name on it! Let's take it higher, girls!

Janey   I can't afford it. What with Steph not working and –

Janice   And nothing. It's paid for. My cousin Cathy dropped out this morning. There's no cancellation policy. Buy her a bottle of wine, Janey. That'll cover it. And anyway, you'll be doing me a favour: I need the back-up.

Janey   You know what? Yeah. Yeah! Why not!

Zumba Instructor   Ladies at the back there. Less chat means less fat! Last warning. Let me see you sweat! Now pump it!

Scene Five

Narrator   Seven p.m. Courtney is sitting staring into space. Like girlfriends, sisters and daughters are doing right now all over the country after reading some 'banter' about themselves online.

Jack   What's up?

Courtney   Sophie 'Steak Bake' McGregor. That's what's up. Sometimes I wish Facebook had never been invented. Slagging me off again. Ma hair. Ma spots.

Jack   Your new hair's great. Sticks and stones, Court.

Courtney   It's okay for you, Jack. You're a boy. When a gang of lassies pick on you, it hurts. Makes you feel so left out. You want to die. Actually die. Throw yourself off a bridge.

Jack   Look at the state of her! When she was a baby her maw must have fed her way a sling.

He mimes firing food from a slingshot.

Splat! She's a blob. I mean, she's the spitting image of Peter Griffin. Don't send a volley back. Speak to her, face to face. Confront her. She'll bottle it.

Courtney   She pulled my hair!

Jack   Aye I know, but what age were you?

Courtney   Six.

Jack   And now you're sixteen and she's sixteen stone, six teeth left and heading for a heart attack. Nip it in the bud face to face.

Courtney   I'll think about it.

Jack   I brought your book back.

He hands **Courtney** *her book. She puts it on the bed beside her.*

Jack   Guess what the main ingredient in black pudding is?

Courtney   Blood?

Jack   On the packet it says hemoglobin. He-mo-fuckin-globin. He-mo-fuckin-boggin', mare like.

He pretends to gag.

James (*shouts*)   Courtney. That's us home!

Jack   You still want those green-and-red high-tops you were talking about?

Courtney   Can't afford them.

Jack   If you help me paint my room I'll chip in.

Courtney   Will ye! I'll pay you back!

James *knocks on the door.*

Courtney   Come in.

James *comes in.*

James   Jack the lad. Here again?

Jack   Yes, Mr –

James   Call me James. I've told you that. Seen your driveway? What's that numpty Steph up to? Looks like Paddy's Market out there.

Jack   He's decorating.

James   Is that what ye call it? He has single-handedly flattened the house prices in this side of the city.

Jack   He's in the middle of doing everything up. Honest.

James   Bet he's trying to get in the good books. Fitba on Sunday. Every man in Glasgow is walking a tightrope so they can get to the pub. DIY centres have never been busier.

He sees the book.

What's this you're reading?

Courtney *picks up the book and throws it to* **Jack**.

Courtney   It's Jack's.

Jack   Is it?!

James   Let's see. Let's see. Is it some kind of crime novel? Wan eh they vampire books? Read that *Da Vinci Code*? Ah couldnay put it doon.

Jack   It's rotten. You, you, you wouldn't –

James   Hey, hey, hey. I'm a reader. Half-dozen books in a wee stack. Sun lounger. Spanish beer on tap. Tapas by the pool. Topless señoritas. Happy as a pig in shit. Int Ah, Courtney?

Courtney   Dad! Jack and me are trying to study.

James   Aye well. As long as it's no biology. Know what I'm saying, Jack?

Jack *forces an embarrassed laugh.* **James** *puts his hand out.*

Jack   Honest. You wouldn't –

James   I'll decide. Looking for a new read. Hand it over.

Jack *gives the book to* **James***, who puts on his reading glasses.*

Courtney   Eh – Jack's writing an essay on 'Teenage Identity'.

Jack   Um Ah?!

Courtney   Aye. Ye ur!

James   Right. Okay. What have we here? (*Reads.*) *It's Okay to Be Different* by Zac Lightfoot. 'A young persons' guide to personal fulfilment. Winner of the Rainbow Medal for Literature 2009.' We live in modern times alright. When I was your age I was still reading *The Victor.*

Jack   I need to go. Need to, to, to, to, to, to, to, to . . . pick paint for my room!

James   No pink I hope.

He hands the book back to **Jack***.*

Take your 'study material' way ye, Jackaline. And go easy on the personal fulfilment. When I was your age we were told too much personal fulfilment could turn a man blind.

Courtney   Daaad!

Scene Six

Split scene.

Narrator   Friday night in both neighbours' kitchens. Must be something in the air 'cause Steph and James have both decided to make dinner. This entails grilling some deed shit and slapping it on some rolls.

Steph   The Hydro?! Two days?

Janey   The shoe is on the other foot. You get to go out with your pals. My turn.

Steph   Thought we were gone to tidy up the gairden nat this weekend?

Janey   Steph, honey, *you* are tidying up the garden. Looks like a scrapyard out there. And the moss on the driveway and on the garage roof needs sorted out. It's a disgrace.

Steph   Go up there? Withoot a harness? I'm scared of heights.

Janey   Scared of work more like.

*

Narrator   James is burning his fingers on the grill. Janice is warming up before going out on a run. Lucky bastart James is grilling square sausages and tomatoes oot a tin. He thinks this makes it a healthy option.

James   You noticed anything funny about Jack?

Janice   Has he took a stretch?

James   Would you say he's maybe . . . at a crossroads in his life? Finding himself?

Janice   What you on about?

James   Do you think he . . . might be finding out who he really is? Which side he bats for?

Janice   He's in a cricket team?

James   For Christsake no! You know what I mean.

Janice   What? Oh. He might be gay?

James   Your words, not mine.

Janice   If he is, he is.

*

Steph   Lucky Ah took the battery out the smoke alarm, eh? That's what you call forward thinking.

Janey   Jack's going to paint his room. Aren't you, sunshine?

Jack   Aye. I'm painting it orange with blue stripes.

Steph   Our ma deed bo-day!

Narrator   Steph slaps the smoking blob of burnt hemoglobin on to a roll and hands it to Jack. Jack looks inside his Morton roll and feels queasy.

Janey   And no winding up the neighbours when I'm away, Steph. I'm not coming back to carnage.

Steph   Aye, aye. Loud and clear. And nay Buckie. Even oot a wine gless. Nay pals roon. This is your hoose, no a bus shelter. Ah know the script.

Narrator   Jack looks inside his roll and gets the mini-boke.

Steph   You no want that, Union? Suhin wrang way it?

Jack   It's burnt.

Steph   Ma Haw Maws. Bit a broon sauce and ye'll be fine.

Jack   Need holy water to save that.

Steph   Saving the holy water for Sunday.

Janey   And that's another thing. We are going to start eating healthy in this house.

Steph   Disnay git mare healthy than a roll own black pud way broon sauce. That's three of your five a day!

Jack *and* **Janey** *cough as smoke fills the room.*

Janey   You trying to smoke the whole place out?!

Steph   If you can't stand the heat get out of the kitchen.

He coughs.

Janey   It's not the heat I'm worried about. Get that out of here, Stephen, please! I can't see!

Steph   Oot ma wiy afore somebody gits hospitalised!

Narrator   Steph grabs the tea towel, with the words to the Soldier Song on it that he bought to wind up the neighbours on the day of the royal wedding, and pulls the grill pan out with a clatter.

All   CLATTER!

Narrator   Steph takes the lard-spitting grill pan out the door and chucks it into the back garden. You can take the bhoy oot the scheme . . .

All   . . . but you can't take the scheme oot the bhoy!

*

Janice   So to cut a long story short – the three of us are going to the Hydro. Sheila's not fit for another bout of Hugh's palaver. I need you to make sure he doesn't go aff his heed when we're away. Phone him the night and get him round tomorrow. Try and talk to him about his behaviour. Go bait fishing or watch a DVD or something. And *don't* go up the Legion. The less pictures of the Queen he sees before the football the better. And I want you to offer to help Steph with the big tidy up. If he doesn't get it done before Janey comes back she'll blow a gasket.

*

Jack   Mam. Can I have a word with you about something? There's something I need to tell you. It's been on my mind. For ages.

Janey   Is it life or death?

Jack   No really; but it's important. To me.

Janey   If it's not life or death it can wait till I'm back.

Jack   It can't wait!

Janey   Okay, okay.

Jack   Look, Mum. Don't know how to tell you this. I've always known I was different. Since I was a wee boy.

Janey   Son. I love you. You can tell me anything.

Jack   Mum . . . It's . . . I'm sorry . . . I hope you can understand.

Narrator   Steph comes in eating two black dods of burnt haemoglobin.

Jack   Mam . . . I think am . . . I think am . . . I think am a vegetarian!

Steph   Yer a veggi-fuckin' whit?

*

James   Is it Bob-a-Job week or something!?

Janice *sings the opening line of the theme tune to* Neighbours.

James   Exactly. And we get Steph!

Janice   We've had worse. Us girls have had enough of running around after your backsides. Listening to rants about penalties and diving. It's boring. Brings out the worst in people.

James   Well, I'm no happy about it.

Janice   Tough.

She turns on her charm.

James . . . mind I'll be getting a wax.

James   Okay. I'm happy about it.

Janice   That doesn't mean you'll get to polish the bonnet.

James   Oh. Gees a kiss, ya sexy wee beauty!

Janice   Git aff me! They sausages are burning.

Narrator   James takes the red, white and blue tea towel with the words to 'God Save the Queen' on it that they bought to celebrate the royal wedding, soaks it under the tap and throws it over the smoking cooker.

All   TTSSS!

Scene Seven

Narrator   Jack's bedroom. Saturday morning, ten a.m. Everything is covered in Courtney's old duvet covers. Courtney and Jack are painting the ceiling. Who says teenagers are lazy!

Jack   Fuck this.

He stops painting.

Narrator   Jack points to a faded blue-and-red duvet cover. In large white lettering. 'Rangers five. Celtic wan.'

Courtney   What's up with you?

Jack   I asked you to bring over some old sheets. No a reminder of the worst day of my life.

Courtney   What you talking about?

Jack   Day ma da left. Last Sunday in November. I was only five. He smashed the telly way a toastie-maker when the fifth goal went in. Melted cheese awe up the wa. Ma mam took me to ma granny's. Ma granny gave me two caramel wafers and her boattle of American Cream Soda. So I knew it was serious.

Courtney   How was I to know? If Steph hadn't used every sheet in this house to mop up that sea of purple gloss I wouldn't have needed to bring them. My Uncle Hugh knew we were using it to catch paint? He'd be beelin'. That's a Christmas present.

Narrator   Jack dunks the roller into the tray of paint and splodges a thick layer of magnolia over the Rangers badge.

Jack   Smell the roller.

Courtney   You're acting like a dick.

They continue to paint in silence. **Courtney** *turns on the radio.*

All *sing the last line of the chorus of 'Saturday Night's Alright for Fighting'.*

Radio Presenter 1   That was 'Saturday Night's Alright for Fighting' by Elton John.

Radio Presenter 2   Aye and a Sunday night efter the football's no so bad either.

Radio Presenter 1   We've had a request in from Sean Michael in Coatbridge.

Radio Presenter 2   All the way from the Little Vatican, eh? (*Sarcastic laugh.*) Sean. What can we do you for?

Sean Michael   Alrighty! Any chance you could play 'Dirty Old Town' by The Pogues fur ma wee boy Henrick, Lubo, Johnstone, McStay; ya pair a Orange–

Radio Presenter 1   Well, Sean Michael seems to have dropped the phone.

Radio Presenter 2   But there's nay chance he'll drop that bottle of Buckie though, eh? Well, no this early onywiy.

Radio Presenter 1   We'll try and look that track out later. In the meantime; this is Leggy Tina Turner with 'Simply the Best'.

All *sing the second line of the chorus of 'Simply the Best'.*

Jack *goes over and turns off the radio.*

Courtney   Hey. That song reminds me of being wee.

She goes over to switch the radio back on. **Jack** *stops her.*

Jack   Naw!

Courtney   If that's the kinda mood you're in, better warn ye: Uncle Hugh is defo coming over tomorrow. So I'm defo watching the game here with you.

Jack   Steph will love that. True Blue Hugh still got that Homer Simpson wearing a sash T-shirt? Diddy. Bringing his flute with him is he?

Courtney   You're just jealous that he can play an instrument.

Jack   A flute is not an instrument.

Courtney   You're an instrument!

Awkward silence.

Jack   Look, Am sorry. I think Am coming down with Old Firm fever. I'll come with you into town the morra. Get the high-tops?

Courtney   I'm gonna pay you back.

Jack   No you won't. You're helping me paint. That's fair. Using the money left to put a deposit down on a . . .

He pretends the paint roller is a guitar.

Dinga-dink. A-dink-dink. Dinga-dink. Der ner!

Courtney   A deposit's one thing – learning to play like Kurt Cobain is another. Uncle Hugh's great at the flute. I used to walk with them. Me, ma mum, Auntie Sheila. Me skipping along at the side. Eating sweeties. Drinking Fanta.

Jack   Had to be feckin' Fanta!

Courtney   And what?

Jack   It's orange. Proddy orange.

Courtney   You're pathetic!

Jack   Hugh's a rocket!

Courtney   So's Steph!

Another awkward silence.

Jack   Court. Know what I was thinking?

Courtney   That you're a bigot?

Jack   Wis a bigot. Am in recovery. That was a relapse. Hingin' about with Steph too much.

Courtney   Better be.

Jack   I'll prove it. See at the end of Old Firm games. At the end. When the whistle goes. The players should swap jerseys. And I don't mean throw them at each other.

Courtney   You being serious?

Jack   Aye. If they can do it after internationals. Actually, officially swap shirts. Know what I mean?

Courtney   OMG, Jay! That's a great idea! Smiley face, smiley face, smiley face. I need to Facebook that!

Jack   Courtney, you would Facebook a silent fart.

Courtney *puts down her brush and takes her phone out.* **Jack** *goes back to painting the ceiling.*

Courtney   Breaking news. Exclamation mark. Seriously. Jack cracks it. Old Firm to swap shirts after each game. Genius or whit. Question mark. Kiss, kiss, kiss. Peace and love. Exclamation mark.

Narrator   Courtney reads the new posts on her Facebook page. A message pops up from Sophie McGrrrrregor.

Sophie McGregor   'Seen Courtney the clown's new look.
Tartan shorts and purple tights? Whit next. Total rid neck
man. HACKIT! L.M.F.A.O. Exclamation mark. Exclamation
mark, exclamation mark. Whit a riot. Her and her Catholic
pal deserve a shunkie for their daft goth pish. Am away tay
Greggs, fur a four-pack a steak bakes. Man, Am pure starvin'.
Yum yum. Peace out. Sophie M.'

Courtney   Pastry munchin' bitch!!

Scene Eight

Narrator   High noon on Saturday.

All   Wah-a-waha-wah. A-wa-wah!

Narrator   Steph is kneeling down by the kitchen steps
cleaning moss off with a brand new wallpaper-scraper. The
September sun is shining. Two magpies fight over the remains
of a burnt black pudding in the back garden.

Steph   This is dane ma feckin' nut in!

Narrator   James is walking back from the shop with a red-
top paper under his arm.

James *is whistling.*

Narrator   He sees Steph. Remembering that he's under
strict instructions to offer to help, he goes over.

James   You seen the day's paper?

Steph   The only thing I've seen is blood, sweat and tears, ma
man.

James   Aye, well, prepare yersel for mare greeting.

He hands **Steph** *the paper.* **Steph** *reads the back page.*

James   Yer new Brazilian wonderkid's crocked. I heard he's
shite. No the first Brazilian *shite* you've signed, eh? Fell coming
out the shower. Probably bending down to pick up the soap.

Steph   Yer feckin' jokin'! And Grand Master Billy Mason's the ref!

He reads more.

And the touchline ban's no been lifted. Surprise sur-feckin-prise. May as well go doon the bookies the noo and put a hunner on two of oor players getting sent aff for dissent and you winning with a penalty that isnay a penalty in the last dying seconds of the game.

James   Oh, here we go. The excuses have started already.

Steph   A penalty that with hindsight will be described in Monday's papers as a blatant dive.

He hands back the newspaper to **James**.

James   How you coping with the missus been away?

Steph   Survivin'.

James   Between me and you, it's nice to have the weekend aff. Nay six-hour trawl roon The Fort the day for me. Big Hugh's coming round for a few beers. Gonnay watch *Walter – Story of a Rangers Legend*. Get ourselves in the mood for the morra.

Steph   Awright for some.

James   You're more than welcome to pop in.

Steph   Is it a comedy?

James   Is a comedy? Am no the wan trying to scrape a quarter tonne of moss aff way a wallpaper-scraper.

Steph   Aye well, needs must. Av a list as long and daft as an Orange Walk. Been at this for at least an oor. Still got the driveway and the garage to go. Never gonnay get through it.

James   Ahl give you a lenny a pressure-washer. You'll have it finished for the bookies shutting.

Steph   Ye sure?

James   Aye. No sweat. That's what neighbours are for.

Steph   Ideal!

Narrator   It's at this point in the story everything starts to go tits up. James goes into his garage and brings out a royal blue pressure-washer.

James   Here ye go. It's Hugh's. It's his pride and joy.

Steph   It's blue!

James   The Prince William Mark Two. The Prince William Mark One was ran over by a dustbin lorry. Shuggie boy sued the council for damage to his emotional well-being 'cause of that.

Steph   It's blue-nose blue!

James   So be careful with it. And Ahl need it back. He'd go aff his heed if he knew I lent it to you.

Steph   That's the bluest thing Av ever seen!

James   If you are gonnay slag it. Forget it.

Steph   Naw, naw. Ahl take a lenny it. Ahl wear my Celtic goalie gloves in case it burns me.

James   Just make sure you don't break it.

Steph   Aye, nay bother, boss. I'll bring it back this efternin. Afore ye go. Know a good place to buy some cheap sheets?

James   Oh that's right. They shut doon Paddy's Market dint they?

Steph   Ha feckin' ha.

James *walks away.*

Steph   If that donkey Hugh starts any of his pish. Al stick this up his arse. And switch it own!

Scene Nine

Narrator   One p.m. on Saturday afternoon. Courtney's back in her bedroom on the phone to her mum.

Courtney   How's the Hydro?

Janice   The place is fabulous. Is Dad helping Steph with the big tidy-up?

Courtney   Aye, I think so. I saw them talking earlier.

Janice   That's good. Can you guess what I'm doing right now?

Courtney   Knitting a scarf?

Janice   I'll knitting a scarf ye! I'm lying by the pool covered in Mediterranean mud from top to toe. Feels fantastic.

Courtney   You having a great time then?

Janice   Nearly. Yer Auntie Sheila's no dane too good. Worried that your Uncle Hugh's going to go off on one if the Rangers get beat. She's locked herself in her room. Says she's got a headache. I'm going up to see her after this. How's things with you?

Courtney   Fine.

Janice   You don't sound fine.

Courtney   It's nothing.

Janice   It's not nothing. I know you like the back of my hand. Now tell me, young lady. What's up?

Courtney   It's just. That Sophie McGregor has been saying things on Facebook. About me. About my hair. What I wear. My spots.

Janice   Bloody Facebook. You don't need to be on it if it is going to upset you.

Courtney   It's not about me being on it. It's about the entire school being on it.

Janice   Do you want me to have a word with her mother?

Courtney   No!

Janice   I can talk to your teachers and –

Courtney   Are you trying to make this worse?! Look, Mum.
I need to go.

Janice   Wait. We should talk. We need to do something
about this.

Courtney   Forget I even mentioned it!

Narrator   Courtney hangs up. She looks out the black
blinds of her bedroom window and sees Sophie McGregor, in
the lumi-white tracky that makes her look like the Marshmallow
Man from *Ghostbusters*. Sophie stops, looks around her to see if
anybody is watching, then grogs a dirty big yella grogger on
the windscreen of James's car.

All   SPLAT!

Narrator   Courtney goes to bang on the glass of her bedroom
window but stops herself. She feels sick. Scared. She looks at
the fresh coat of black nail-polish she had applied this morning.
She sits down on edge of her bed and starts to pick it off.

Scene Ten

Narrator   One hour later. Jack covered in paint. Looks like
he's just been shat on from a very high height by a ten-tonne
pigeon. Jack is in the kitchen making toast and peanut butter
for him and Courtney before they slap on the third coat. Steph
is outside, standing in the middle of a mass of tangled cables.
He is soaked in sweat from all the 'hard work' he's been doing.
He checks the pressure-washer is plugged into the extension
cable. The kitchen window is open – one end of a garden hose
is connected to the hot tap. The other end is plugged into the
Price William.

Steph   Union! Union! Throw me a can oot, Union. Party starts here.

Jack   Keep your goalie gloves on! Bit early for boozin', is it no?

Steph   Whit! Look. Av been up since Dawn's crack. Am nearly finished.

Jack   You've only started!

Steph   You're whit they call wan of they gless half empty cants. Me? Am wan they gless half full cants. But right noo ma glass is empty. So chuck us oot a can, ya wee cant!

Narrator   Jack leans out the window and lobs Steph a can of TL.

Steph   Some man! Am gonnay blast the kate aff the roof an that's us. Well, still need to scrape awe the wee fiddly bits roon the back steps.

Jack draws **Steph** a look.

Jack   And?!

Steph   Eh, plant they bulbs nat.

Jack   And?

Steph   Get rid awe they tyres.

Jack   And?

Steph   Burn they three Christmas trees fay the last three Christmases.

Jack   Nearly there.

Steph   And take they two hunner Ba Bru bottles back tay the shoaps. Satisfied? You're worse than yer maw.

Jack   Mind I've saw the list. It's written in red pen. In capitals!

Steph   Aye, aye. Noo, lit me get back to the kate.

Jack   Kate?

Steph   Aye. The kate, man. Cockney rhyming slang int it. Kate. Kate Moss.

Jack   That doesn't rhyme.

Steph   Aye it dis, ya wee bawbag.

Jack   Fine.

Steph   Put the radio on, Union. Turn it up. I'm gonnay get right into this.

Narrator   Steph throws the pressure washer on to the flat garage roof and pulls open the can of lager. Takes a long hard jake-dog swalley. Gulps it down.

Steph *burps.*

Narrator   He slides the half can on to the moss-matted garage roof. Climbs up.

Jack   Am away up the stairs to finish this painting. Cash in hand?

Steph   I'm no gonnay put it through the books um Ah? Money's in ma back poacket.

Jack   I need it the day.

Narrator   Jack turns on the radio.

Radio Presenter 1   There's a wee nip in the air but that won't stop all the Old Firm fans trying to get into the good books with the wife before tomorrow's clash. Says in the day's paper statistically there's more grass gets cut today than any other day of the year!

Radio Presenter 2   That's right, Charlie. I read that. And let's hope Rangers get into these. I mean, let's hope tomorrow's game is remembered for all the right reasons.

Steph (*doing his best Tony Montana impersonation*)   You wanna fuck with me? Okay. You wanna play rough? Okay. Say hello to my little friend!

All of the **Cast** *make the purring sound of pressure washers.*

All   PPPPPPRRRRRR!

Narrator   Steph pulls the trigger, the power purr of the machine vibrates like a machine gun in his hands. The moss massacre begins. He feels the control surge in his veins. The power. It feels good. Too good.

Scene Eleven

Narrator   Three thirty p.m. Saturday afternoon at the Hydro. Janey and Janice, wrapped up in crisp terry-towelling, are lording it in the conservatory. Surrounded by deep-green yukka plants; teardrop crystals hang from the ceiling emitting a hundred spectrums of colour over the whiteness of their luxury robes. Janice is reading the paper.

Janey   Maybe I shouldn't have stayed in the pool that long. I can feel it in my shoulders.

Janice   No pain, no gain.

Janey *looks at the picture on the front of the paper.*

Janey   Is that Tom Cruise falling off a jet-ski?

Janice   Hm?

Janey   Between you and me, I wouldnay mind doing the deep down and dirty doggy paddle way that sexy wee midget.

Janice   Hm?

Janey   I said. Doesn't matter. What you reading about?

Janice   Says in today's paper. Women are twice as likely to suffer domestic violence after an Old Firm game and three times as likely when the game is played on a holiday weekend.

Janey   Doesn't bear thinking about.

Janice   We can't keep sweeping it under the carpet.

Janey   What did Sheila say when you went up?

Janice   She wouldn't come to the door. I think it's worse than she's letting on.

Janey   It's always worse. It's always the tip of the iceberg.

Janice   We're lucky.

Janey   Jack thinks his dad left me. He never. I kicked him out. If they do it once, trust me, they do it again.

Janice   Janey, I never . . . Want to talk about it?

Janey   It's not always football and drink, Janice. But it's always about control. Could be that his egg wasn't sunny-side up or I'd forgot to change the batteries in the remote for the telly. It's not always a fist. The shouting's just as scary. Spit hitting your cheek, going in your eye. Bad breath in your ear. The pushing and the shove-shove-shoving. Where have you been? Bitch this. Lazy that.

Janice   Janey, I don't know what to say.

Janey   Steph, for all his faults, has been good to me – good *for* me. Makes me laugh. I never thought I'd be able to relax in a man's company again. I'll go up and speak to Sheila. We're here to have a good time.

Narrator   A bronzed Australian waiter arrives with a basket of hot stones and a wine list.

Waiter   Hot stones, madam?

Janey   That's great. You can put them just there.

Waiter   And was it a bottle of Spanish or Portuguese rosé you ordered, madam?

Janice   What time's it?

Janey   Just after half three.

Janey *and* **Janice**   Both!

Waiter   You saucy little koalas.

Scene Twelve

Narrator   Saturday three forty-five p.m. At this time tomorrow the game will be over and the stadium empty. But the pubs won't be. And whatever the score, Casualty will just be warming up. Women like Sheila, from both sides of the city, will be sitting in their kitchens worrying. Praying for it to stop. Courtney is looking at an old Celtic scarf covered in badges. Old metal badges of every shape imaginable. Jack comes in with a leaning tower of toast.

Jack   Watch you don't get paint on it!

Courtney   I'm being careful. Look at the stitching. You've never showed me this? My granda's got a scarf like this.

She gives **Jack** *the Celtic scarf and she is handed a Rangers one by a member of the* **Cast***. The next section is direct address to the audience.*

Jack   My granny gave me it. The day my da left. It was her scarf. She wore it at every home game before she had to stop going. That scarf tells a story. 'A supporter's story,' she said.

Courtney   This is ma granda's scarf. Some of the badges on it are sewn on. Like Boys' Brigade badges.

Jack   Folk saved up every week to go to the fitba she told me. People would walk for miles to get to the games. Take a jam or cheese piece wrapped in brown paper, quarter of liquorice and water out the tap in a ginger bottle.

Courtney   He keeps it in a cabinet in the living room. He keeps his da's, ma great granda's, war medals in it tay. And a boattle whiskey fay nineteen canteen shaped like a big golf ball that he thinks husnay been opened. But see, I know it's filled way tea 'cause ma da and uncle Hugh drank it when we goat nine in a row.

Jack   That scarf's been all over, she said. Even been to the Estádio Nacionale, Lisbon.

Courtney   This scarf. Worth its weight in gold. Last day ma granda wore it was at the Ibrox Disaster.

Jack   Ma granny said, 'Jack, I never have had the money to get to the final. Never had the money to go anywhere. I've never even been to Butlins in Ayr. But my cousin Bill, he took this scarf with him, on the supporters' bus.' So this scarf got to all the big games.

Courtney   Granda says it will take a lot for him to wear it again. Out of respect for the people who died on that freezing cold night. Priests and ministers went roon the doors the gither, to help the victims of the families. Said the city was brought together that night by grief.

Jack   'It's your scarf now, Jack. I'm sorry things haven't worked out with your mum and your dad,' she said.

Courtney   Says that he hopes one day this city will be brought together by respect; happiness; understanding. Until then. That blue scarf, with the wee sewn on badges, stays in the cabinet.

Jack   These days. Look at Steph. Folk buy three new scarves a season. Leaving them at their arse on buses, taxis, benches in beer gardens when they're pished. Disposable. But scarves like these, Court. All they memories. Means something. Know whit Ah mean? Scarves like these.

Courtney   Scarves like these are for life.

Narrator   Steph is on the garage roof having a private party with Prince William.

All *sing the opening line of the chorus of Lionel Richie's 'Dancing on the Ceiling'.*

Steph   Pressure-washing on the ceilin'.

All *sing it again.*

Steph   Celtic winning. Rangers will be beelin'.

Narrator   The moss and muck lifts in long strips and splatters on to the driveway. Steph starts to dance around. Takes another long hard swalley and drains his third can of TL.

Radio Presenter 3   Sunny Govan FM. Where the classics keep coming. That song was for the men in blue just round the corner. Lionel Ritchie with that eternal classic, 'Dancing on the Ceiling'. What Govan, I mean Glasgow, football team will be dancing on the ceiling tomorrow afternoon? We'll soon see.

Narrator   Steph notices the cable of the pressure washer is caught on the corner of the garage roof.

Radio Presenter 3   This one's for the boys in the East End. This is Smokey Robinson and the Miracles with 'Tears of a Clown'. Get it right up ye!

Steph   You're the clown ya blue sack!

Narrator   Steph yanks the cable of the Prince William, accidentally catapulting the machine off the roof. Like a fridge falling out of a skyscraper. It twists and turns in the afternoon air. Steph turns round in slowed-down slow motion. The proud blue Prince William Mark Two smashes into smithereens on the driveway.

We hear the loud smash of the machine hitting the ground.

Steph   Naaaaaaawwwww!!

Narrator   Back in the bedroom, Jack and Courtney hear the smash. They run down the stairs and out on to the driveway. Steph jumps off the roof and lands on his arse. He's winded.

Jack   Steph, man. Look what you've done!

Steph   Am windit!

Courtney   Uncle Hugh's Prince William!

Jack   You'll be mare than winded when ma maw gets a hod eh ye!

Courtney   My Uncle Hugh loves that machine! Takes it on holiday with him to their caravan in Saltcoats and everything. He'll be ragin'!

Steph   Was an accident.

Jack   What you gonnay day, Steph?!

Steph   Looks like Al need to buy the hun a feckin new wan, dint it!

Courtney   Less of the hun!

Narrator   Amiable James runs out to see what all the noise is about and clocks the carcass of the once proud Prince William Mark Two spread across the driveway.

James   Please tell me that's not what I think it is.

Jack   Was an accident. He didnay mean –

James   Was it? Was it really? What did Ah say, Steph? You trying to pish doon ma leg?

Courtney   Dad!

Steph   Who you talking tay? You talking tay me?

Jack   Steph – stoap it!

Steph   I never fuckin' started it!

James   Aye ye bloody did!

Scene Thirteen

Narrator   Saturday teatime. Hands have been shaken, then cold looks drawn. James and Hugh are in the living room watching *Walter – Story of a Rangers Legend*.

James   Another can of amber nectar, Shug?

Hugh   Why not, Jamesy? What do you think, Walter? A wee can to celebrate old times?

James   There's one thing that you can say for Walter Smith. Not only is he a tactical genius. That man is a gentleman. A true gentleman. An ambassador for the game.

Hugh   Aye. Unlike some. Where's wee Courtney?

James   She's away into the toon to buy some new high-tops. Trainers to you and me.

Hugh   Red, white and blue wans, one hopes. Way a Union Jack on the toe for booting Fenians up the arse.

James   Easy does it, Hugh. It's no the morra yet! She says there's no point going into town when the game's on. Says she'd rather take her chances in the Middle East than go shopping on the day of an Old Firm clash.

Hugh   Bloody Celtic fans. They're the problem. And you know why that is? They're awe own the dole. I mean the famine's over. They should go back to Ireland and sign on the paddy bru.

James   Ah come on, Hugh. There's no need for that kinda talk.

Hugh   The truth hurts, Jamesy boy. That Steph next door goat a job yet?

James   Don't think so.

Hugh   I rest my case. Meant to ask: you finished with the Prince William? With Sheila being away I thought Ad wash ma motor in the mornin'. Keep the butterflies doon before we molicate the antichrist's eleven the morra!

James   Oh. Right. Well. Em. Aye, I need to talk to you about that.

Narrator   Courtney comes in with a big cardboard box in a bin bag and a shoe box in a plastic sports bag over her shoulder.

Courtney   Hiya, Uncle Hugh.

Hugh   How's my favourite Rangers supporter?

Courtney   Just fine, Uncle Hugh. Still coming round to watch the game tomorrow?

Hugh   Naw. Since your Auntie Sheila thinks it's okay to swan off and abandon us. I used three hunner pound of our Crete money to buy your dad and me tickets. Bought them aff the internet. Canny wait. That's some pair of shoes you must have bought!

Courtney   Don't be daft. This is for my dad. Steph asked me to bring it over. Here's my new shoes here.

She holds out the plastic sports bag.

Hugh   Let's see them then. Nay green in them, I hope!

Courtney   They're red . . . red and aquamarine. I'm in a hurry.

Hugh   Aquamarine? Gone swimming in them?

Courtney *gives* **James** *the bin bag.*

James   Thanks, honey. Where you off to now?

Courtney   Just going over to Jack's to help him finish painting his room.

James   Okay doke.

Hugh (*shouts*)   Courtney, mind the Walter Smith DVD's here if you want to watch it later.

Courtney (*shouts*)   That's great. I will. (*Whispers.*) Steph said for me to tell you. The one he went for was out of stock. This is a better model. More features or something boring like that.

Narrator   James looks in the bag to see a photograph of a bright green pressure-washer staring up at him.

James   Christ on a bloody bike!

Courtney   What's the matter?

James   It's shamrock green!

Courtney   But it's a better model.

Hugh (*shouts*)   What's your prediction?

Courtney (*shouts*)   A draw will suit me.

Hugh (*shouts*)   A draw?! There's more chance of the next Pope being . . . Argentinian than a draw! Courtney, here you heard the wan about the the Pope and the polar bear?

James   That's enough of that, Hugh.

Hugh   Where's your sense of humour!

Courtney   Need to run. Bye, Dad! See you later, Uncle Hugh.

Hugh   See you later, hen. And don't forget.

He makes a W-sign with his thumbs and forefingers.

We are the people!

Feeling she has to, **Courtney** *makes a W-sign back*

Courtney   Aye. We ur.

She exits.

James   Back in a minute, Shug.

Hugh   You look awe flustered. What's in the bag? A deed body?

James   Might be worse than that.

Narrator   James takes the ticking time bomb out to the garage. Hugh's attention is drawn back to the TV.

Hugh   Whit a goal! Get intay these Taig bastarts! Super Ally McCoist does it again!

Scene Fourteen

Narrator   As Courtney pulls her front door closed on her Uncle's Hugh's pish she sees her reflection in the glass. Her new Jolly Roger hair clip looks cool set into her new Goth hair. She smiles to herself and turns round.

All   BANG!

Narrator   There she is. Sophie McGrrrrrrrrrrregor. At the bottom of Courtney's driveway. In her space and in her face. So close that Courtney can smell the remnants of a macaroni pie stuck to her teeth and tongue.

Sophie   Hiya, Courtney. Whit's been happ'nin'? You pregnant yit?

Narrator   Courtney's blood chills. Her mouth dries. Little electric shocks of fear start to tingle behind her kneecaps.

Sophie   I like your tights. Whit colour ur they? Ur they purple? I like your hair clip. Is that new?

Courtney   What do you want?

Sophie   Ma maw says I'm getting fat. She says, 'I'm gonnay feed you lettuce,' but I say ye need need a cushion for the pushin'. Ye get me? How come you're so skinny?

Courtney   I don't eat anything beige.

Sophie   Whit?

Courtney   Forget it.

Sophie   Whit you dane for the fitba?

Courtney   Watching it with Jack. Where you watching it?

Sophie   I won't be. Av a new boyfriend. Ten weeks, four days, sixteen hours. He's in the TA. Prefers watching the rugby. So Am no intay fitba any mare. Am intay shaggin'!

Courtney   And?

Sophie   How come you've no goat a real boyfriend?

Courtney   Maybe it's because I'm a weirdo.

Sophie   You said it. Smelt it, dealt it. Laters.

She begins to waddle away.

Narrator   The little electric shocks of fear that started behind her kneecaps dig into her thighs and scratch the back of her neck. She remembers what Jack said:

Jack (*voice*)   Speak to her, face to face. Confront her. She'll bottle it.

Courtney   Sophie!

Narrator   Sophie turns round slowly. That's 'cause she canny turn roon fast.

Courtney   Is your second name McGregor or McGroger?

Sophie   Whit did you say tay me?

Courtney   You heard.

Sophie   You're lucky Am in a hurry.

Courtney   Gone tay Greggs?

Sophie   Mibay.

Courtney   Anything else you want to say to me, pie-muncher?

Sophie   Naw. How? Shoulda?

Courtney   If you've got anything to say to me, or about me, say it.

Sophie   Whit you own?

Courtney   Say it now. To my face.

Sophie   Are you disrespecting me?

Courtney   Say it!

Sophie   You stiy away fay me.

Courtney   Say it!

Sophie   If you come any closer Ahl phone the polis.

Courtney   If you say anything about me on Facebook or anywhere else again, trust me, you will need to phone the police. But not before I phone you an ambulance. I'll take

your dial aff if you don't stop slagging me behind my back.
Think I cannay read, Sophie? If you've got something to say,
say it to my face.

Sophie *backs away.*

Courtney   Where do you think you're gone, McGroger?

Sophie   You're a weirdo head case. I'm phoning the polis!

Courtney   Phone them! The number's 999.

Narrator   Courtney feels adrenaline shake through her
veins. Scared. Ready to scratch, punch, bite, fight back.

Sophie   Don't you worry. Ahl phone thum.

Courtney   Aye. Efter you've cleaned that big grogger aff
ma da's motor.

Sophie   Whit ye talkin' aboot?

Courtney   Ah saw ye! In fact I filmed ye. Seen the wan on
YouTube way the woman, the cat and the wheelie bin? Public
enemy number one? You're next: 'Sophie McGrogger.
Minger. Caught in Action Grogging on Neighbour's Motor.'
And I'll send a link to the whole school, your imaginary
boyfriend and YOUR MAW!

Sophie   Wisnay me!

Courtney   Clean it!

Narrator   Sophie uses her white tracky sleeve to clean off
the hardening splat of grog.

All   Nice!

Sophie   Ahl sue you if you YouTube me!

Courtney   Whatever.

Narrator   Courtney turns and walks towards Jack's. Filled
with teen spirit, she feels like she's gliding through the air. She
sees Steph dripping sweat outside scraping splashes of masonry
paint off the full-length glass of the kitchen door. James is

walking towards Steph holding the brand new bright-green pressure-washer at arm's length. Like it's a diseased and radioactive lump of carcinogenic trouble.

James   Are you aff yer bloody heed!

Steph   Whit's your problem noo?!

James   *This* is my bloody problem. You trying to take the pish?!

Steph   Cool your feckin' jets. Yer lucky Ah goat that! Last wan in the shop. And the model up. That's the Duke of Edinburgh, by the way. Thirty quid dearer than the Prince William. It's even goat a turbo booster own it. That is top-of-the-range. Simply the best, James!

James   Could you no just buy him the same wan?!

Steph   There were nane left! Awe you orange fuds musts boat thum! Fitba the morra. DIY day, int it!

James   It's bright green! Could you no jist buy him a blue one, or a red one, or a fuckin' tartan wan even?!

Steph   Bite ma banger. The receipt's in the box.

Narrator   Steph points the new wallpaper-scraper menacingly at James. It glints in the sun like a ninja throwing star.

Steph   If it's that big a deal, Shuugie boy can take it back – in his stupit royal-blue motor, way that stupit nodding dug, way the stupit Union Jack waistcoat. And he kin keep the fuckin' chinge!

Hugh *appears just in time to hear* **Steph***'s rant.*

James   Oh whit!

Hugh   Haw, arsehole! You goat a problem with me?! Stonin' thare sweating like a papist.

James   Look, Hugh. Hod your horses. I don't want this getting out of hand.

Narrator   Sophie, leaning against James's motor, is loving it! She's so intay watching the argument that she smears the end of her nose with the sleeve she's just used to wipe up the congealed grogger. She dials the cops.

Courtney   What are you doing! Stop it! Stop fighting. Over nothing!

Sophie   Smash um, big man! Git the knife aff um! Aye. Aye. That the polis? You're needed. Pronto!

Narrator   Jack, splattered in blobs of emulsion paint, has heard the commotion and runs downstairs.

Jack   What the hell's happenin'?!

Steph *holds the wallpaper-scraper in his hand like a chib.*

Steph   Sweating like a whit? Hink yer hard hun chops?

James   Put that doon, Steph! This has gone far enough!

Hugh   Aye. Put it doon. An Ahl show you how hard ah um.

Narrator   The kitchen door with its full-length pane of glass is locked from the outside. Jack tries frantically to pull it open.

Jack   Steph! Steph! Listen tay may!

Courtney   Uncle Hugh! Stop it! Dad!

James   Look, Hugh. Steph accidentally broke your pressure-washer. He bought this wan. It's no the same. But we can sort this out.

Hugh   It's bright fuckin' green!

James   The receipt's in the box, Hugh.

Steph   And whit, ya hun bastart!

James   We can exchange it!

Narrator   Hugh looks down at the bright-green Duke of Edinburgh and red, white and blue mist fills his head. He can hear the pressure of his blood pumping through his body.

James   We can sort this out!

Hugh   Aye, we'll sort it oot aweright!!

He picks up the Duke of Edinburgh and holds it above his head.

Steph   Try it!

Hugh   Fuckin' Fenian fanny!

Narrator   The heavy plastic and metal machine is launched at Steph.

Courtney   Naw Uncle Hugh! Please! Dad, do something!

Narrator   Steph instinctively ducks and the heavy green missile crashes into the full-length pain of glass of the kitchen door. Jack's hand is yanking on the chipped white handle as the plate glass shatters.

James   Jack – watch!

We hear the smash of the pressure-washer as it crashes through the glass door.

Narrator   The three-stone Duke of Edinburgh and a pound of sharp glass shards smashes hard into young Jack's face. There's blood. Lots and lots of blood.

Jack *falls to the ground holding his face.*

Jack   I canny see, Court. I canny see!

Courtney (*screams*)   Jack! Jack!

*She holds **Jack** in her arms.*

Courtney (*shouts*)   Look! Look what you've done. Fitba? Fans? Banter? Bastards! Stupid bastards. You're pathetic! A disgrace to the clubs. A disgrace to your families. As bad as each other. Look what you've done! Don't jist ston there like three spare pricks. Somebody phone a fuckin' ambulance!

Sound of a police siren.

Glossary

a lenny   *a loan of*
a pure roastin'   *being shouted at*
a rocket   *a fool that thinks he is clever*
aff   *off*
aff ma da's motor   *off my dad's car*
aff yer bloody heed   *crazy*
afore   *before*
Ah   *I*
Ahl   *I will*
Ah um   *I am*
Am   *I am*
an nat   *and that*
antichrist's eleven   *derogatory term for the Celtic team*
auld   *old*
Av   *I've*
aw   *all*
awfy   *very*

Ba Bru   *Barr's Irn Bru*
banging the ching   *snorting cocaine*
banter   *activities or conversation that is playful and original*
bawbag   *ball-bag*
beelin'   *really angry*
big grogger   *large lump of phlegm*
bint   *derogatory term for a girl or woman*
bite ma banger   *stop annoying me*
blue-nose   *Rangers fan*
boat thum   *bought them*
bobby-dazzler   *a striking individual*
broon   *brown*
buckie   *Buckfast Tonic Wine*
by the way   *a phrase indicating that the speaker is adding information*

cannay   *can't*
cheeky wee huaf   *a measure of spirits*
chinge   *change*
Coatbridge   *seen as predominately Catholic area in North Lanarkshire*

coont   *count*
Cortonvale   *HMP Cortonvale, the primary establishment in Scotland for holding female offenders remanded or sentenced to prison by the courts*
couldnay put it doon   *couldn't put it down*
cushion for the pushin'   *a belly*

da   *dad, father*
dane   *doing*
Davie Cooper   *famous Rangers player*
day   *do*
diddy   *fool*
dint   *doesn't*
disnay   *doesn't*
doactur   *doctor*
dods   *lumps*
drouf   *severe thirst*
dug   *dog*
fella   *man*

Fenians   *originally used to describe members of the Fenian Brotherhood and the Irish Republican Brotherhood. The term is used today, especially in Northern Ireland and Scotland, as a demeaning term for to include all supporters of Irish Nationalism, Irish Catholics and Celtic supporters*
fitba   *football*
fuckin' Fenian fanny   *derogatory term for a Catholic*
fuds   *plural of Scottish slang term for fool*

gairden   *garden*
gairden nat   *the garden and other chores*
geme   *game*
git aff me   *get off me*
git pished   *get drunk*
gless   *glass*
gonnay   *going to*
grogging   *spitting*
grogs a dirty big yella grogger   *spits phlegm*

hackit   *really ugly*
hame   *home*
haw   *hey*
haw maws   *rhyming slang for baws (testicles)*
heed   *head*
Henrick, Lubo, Johnstone, McStay   *famous Celtic players*
hingin'   *hanging*
hings aboot way   *hangs around with*
hink yer hard?   *do you think you're tough?*
hudnay   *hadn't*
hump the gers   *beat Rangers*
hun   *derogatory term for a Protestant*
hun bastart   *derogatory term for a Protestant*
hun chops   *derogatory term for a Protestant*
hunner   *hundred*
husnay   *hasn't*

Ibrox Disaster   *when sixty-six football supporters were killed following a match between Celtic and Rangers at the Ibrox Park stadium in Glasgow on 2 January 1971. The disaster occurred when crush barriers collapsed as thousands of fans made their way out of the stadium*
int Ah   *aren't I*
intay   *into*

Jimmy Johnstone   *famous Celtic player*
jist ston   *just stand*

kin   *can*
kin Ah git ma phone back noo?   *can I have my phone back now?*

LMFAO   *laughing my fucking ass off*
lassies   *girls*
lumi-white   *luminous white*

ma ane   *my own*
maw   *mum*
mibay   *maybe*
minger   *smelly person*

munchie boax   *a west of Scotland smorgasbord that varies from town to town but usually comprises chips, doner meat, mixed pakora and limp salad all served together in a pizza box*

nane   *none*
naw   *no*
nay   *no*
nay pals roon   *no friends round*
ned   *non-educated delinquent*
nippy-nippy ring-sting sauce   *dangerously spicy dipping sauce*
no   *not*
no dane   *not doing*
noo   *now*

OMFG   *Oh My Fucking God*
onywiy   *anyway*
oor   *hour*
oot aweright   *out alright*
oot eh   *out of*
oot ma wiy afore somebody gits hospitalised   *out of my way before someone gets hospitalised*
orange fuds   *derogatory term for a member of the Orange order or more generally a Rangers supporter*

paddy bru   *Irish social security*
Paddy's Market   *famous Glasgow market started by Irish immigrants*
People's fuckin' Palace   *People's Palace and Winter Gardens in Glasgow, a museum and glasshouse situated in Glasgow Green, opened on 22 January 1898*
Peter Griffin   *main character in the cartoon series* Family Guy
pie-eyed   *very drunk*
pish   *nonsense*
pish doon ma leg   *take advantage of*
pishin' way rain   *raining heavily*
plukey   *riot*
poacket   *pocket*
Polemont   *Scotland's national holding facility for young offenders aged between 16 and 21 years of age*
polis   *Strathclyde Police*

proddy   *derogatory term for a Protestant*
puffin' on some cooncil   *smoking cheap cannabis resin*
puggie   *fruit machine*
pure fuckin' dick   *see arsehole*

rank rotten   *disgusting*
roon   *around*

shite   *Rafael Felipe Scheidt: an infamous Celtic signing that cost a lot of money*
shite   *rubbish*
shoaps   *shops*
Shuggie/Shuugie   *Scottish name for Hugh*
shunkie   *having your underwear pulled up by someone else*
skitters   *diarrhoea*
smash um   *punch him*
smelt it, dealt it   *when a person breaks wind and is the first to mention the smell as a way of covering their guilt*
Soldier Song   *Irish national anthem*
stiy   *stay*
stoap   *stop*
stonin' thare   *standing there*
stupit   *stupid*
suhin wrang way it   *something wrong with it*
Super Ally   *Ally McCoist was a famous Rangers player who is now the manager of the club*
swalley   *gulp*

TL   *Tennant's lager*
Taig   *a derogatory term for an Irish Catholic. It is mainly used by sectarian loyalists in Northern Ireland and Scotland*
take the pish   *make a fool of*
take your dial aff   *to assault and cause facial injury*
tap   *a garment worn on the upper body*
tay   *to*
tay may   *to me*
ten pinter   *heavy drinking session*
the bhoys   *Celtic supporters*
The Corinthian   *a Glasgow restaurant and nightclub*

the gither   *together*
the hoops   *Celtic Football Club*
the morra   *tomorrow*
the toon   *Glasgow city centre*
this is dane ma feckin' nut in   *this is doing my head in*
tinna gloss bastart   *tin of gloss bastard*
total jake dog bastart   *alcoholic*
trackies   *tracksuit*

Union   *Union Jack*
ur   *are*
wa   *wall*
wan   *one*
wan eh they   *one of those*

We are the people   *phrase used by Rangers supporters to show they see themselves as the indigenous people of Scotland*
wean   *child*
whit kinda patter   *what kind of language*
whit   *what*
widnay   *wouldn't*
windit   *winded*
wis   *was*
wis me thit phont the polis   *I was the one that called the police*
wisnay   *wasn't*

Yas!   *a celebratory exclamation*
ye   *you*
ye git may?   *do you understand what I'm saying?*
ye ur   *you are*
yowl-day   *celebratory exclamation*